TYRANNOSAURUS REX
AND ITS KIN

First Edition   1 2 3 4 5 6 7 8 9 10

Library of Congress Cataloging-in-Publication Data   Sattler, Helen Roney. Tyrannosaurus rex and its kin: the Mesozoic monsters / by Helen Roney Sattler.
        p.   cm.   Bibliography: p.   Summary: Discusses the fossil remains, probable appearance, and possible behavior of the gigantic flesh-eating dinosaurs of the Mesozoic, including Tyrannosaurus rex, Allosaurus, and such lesser known relatives as Acrocanthosaurus and Baryonyx walkeri.
ISBN 0-688-07747-1. ISBN 0-688-07748-X (lib. bdg.)   1. Saurischia—Juvenile literature. 2. Paleontology—Mesozoic—Juvenile literature.   [1. Tyrannosaurus rex. 2. Allosaurus. 3. Dinosaurs.] I. Powzyk, Joyce Ann, ill. II. Title. QE862.S3S37   1989   567.9'7—dc19   88-1577 CIP AC

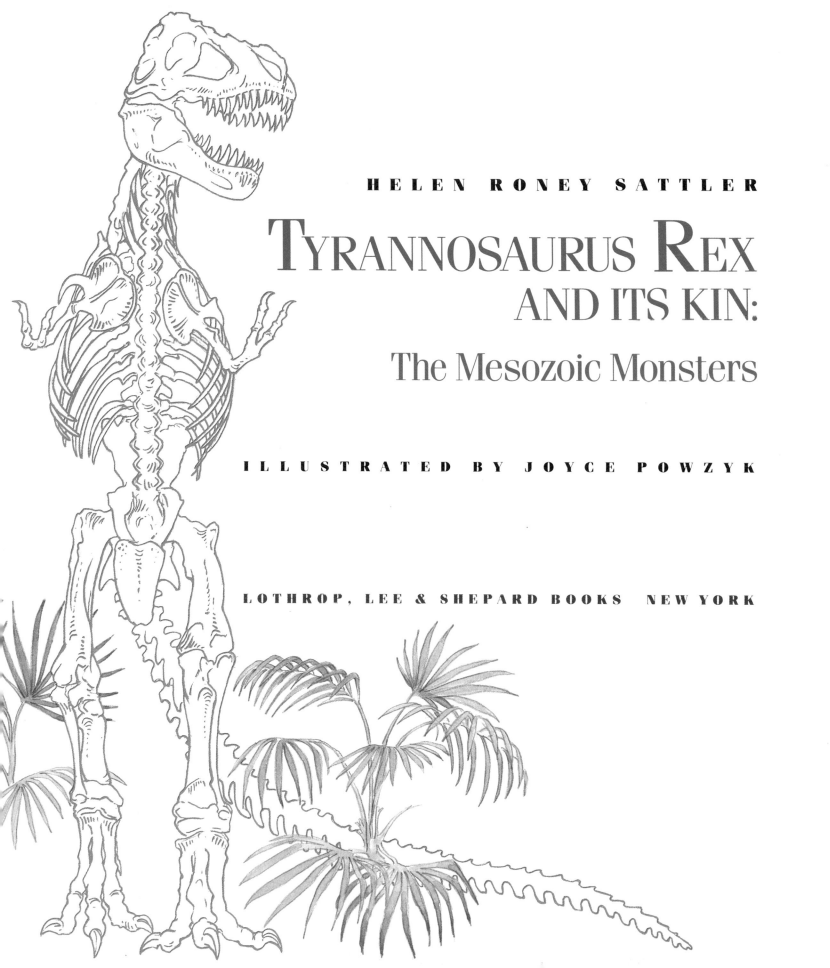

HELEN RONEY SATTLER

TYRANNOSAURUS REX
AND ITS KIN:
The Mesozoic Monsters

ILLUSTRATED BY JOYCE POWZYK

LOTHROP, LEE & SHEPARD BOOKS   NEW YORK

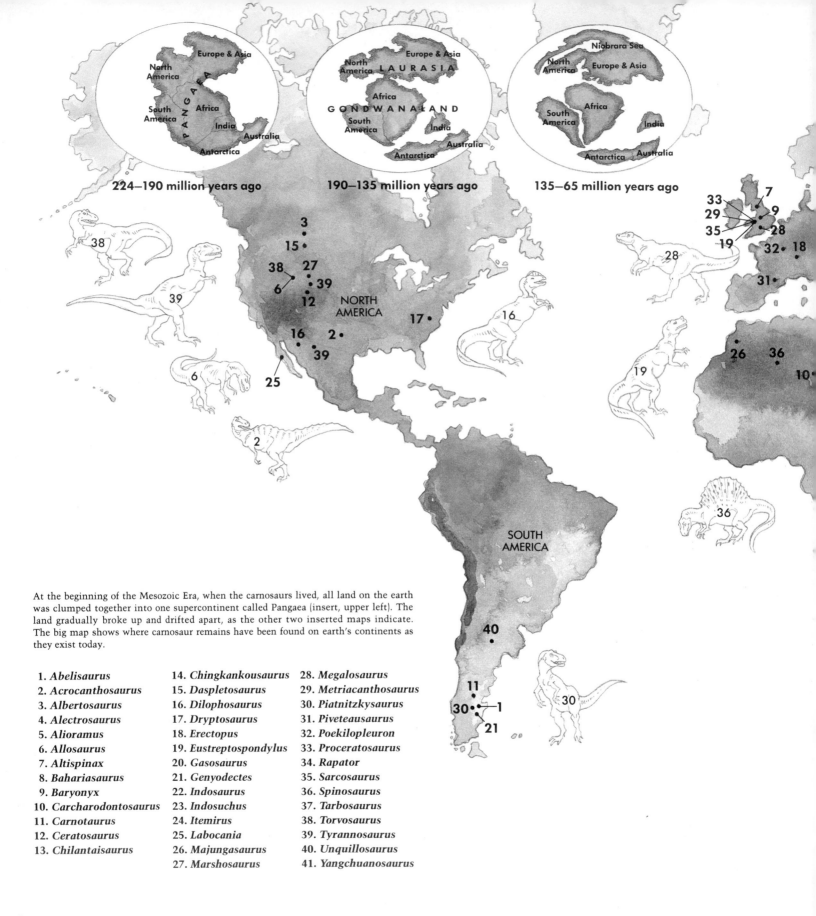

At the beginning of the Mesozoic Era, when the carnosaurs lived, all land on the earth was clumped together into one supercontinent called Pangaea (insert, upper left). The land gradually broke up and drifted apart, as the other two inserted maps indicate. The big map shows where carnosaur remains have been found on earth's continents as they exist today.

1. *Abelisaurus*	14. *Chingkankousaurus*	28. *Megalosaurus*
2. *Acrocanthosaurus*	15. *Daspletosaurus*	29. *Metriacanthosaurus*
3. *Albertosaurus*	16. *Dilophosaurus*	30. *Piatnitzkysaurus*
4. *Alectrosaurus*	17. *Dryptosaurus*	31. *Piveteausaurus*
5. *Alioramus*	18. *Erectopus*	32. *Poekilopleuron*
6. *Allosaurus*	19. *Eustreptospondylus*	33. *Proceratosaurus*
7. *Altispinax*	20. *Gasosaurus*	34. *Rapator*
8. *Bahariasaurus*	21. *Genyodectes*	35. *Sarcosaurus*
9. *Baryonyx*	22. *Indosaurus*	36. *Spinosaurus*
10. *Carcharodontosaurus*	23. *Indosuchus*	37. *Tarbosaurus*
11. *Carnotaurus*	24. *Itemirus*	38. *Torvosaurus*
12. *Ceratosaurus*	25. *Labocania*	39. *Tyrannosaurus*
13. *Chilantaisaurus*	26. *Majungasaurus*	40. *Unquillosaurus*
	27. *Marshosaurus*	41. *Yangchuanosaurus*

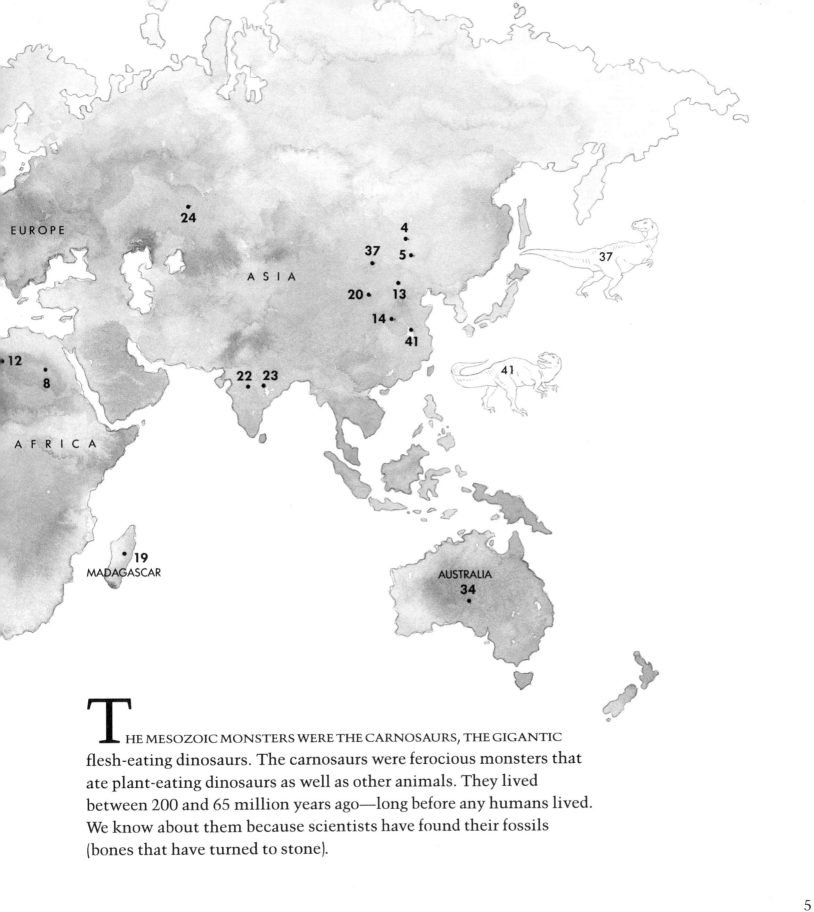

EUROPE

ASIA

AFRICA

•24

•4
37• 5•

20• 13•

14•

41•

22 23
• •

•12

•8

•19
MADAGASCAR

AUSTRALIA
34
•

37

41

T HE MESOZOIC MONSTERS WERE THE CARNOSAURS, THE GIGANTIC
flesh-eating dinosaurs. The carnosaurs were ferocious monsters that
ate plant-eating dinosaurs as well as other animals. They lived
between 200 and 65 million years ago—long before any humans lived.
We know about them because scientists have found their fossils
(bones that have turned to stone).

Carnosaurs lived on every continent except Antarctica. They were the largest land-dwelling predators (animals that kill other animals) that ever lived. The largest predators living today are lions, tigers, and Kodiak bears. A lion is ten feet long from tip of nose to tip of tail, half as long as the smallest Mesozoic monster. Carnosaurs were twenty to fifty feet long and were very dangerous animals. They probably killed only when they were hungry, like most predators of today, but they

Kodiak bears   *Tyrannosaurus rex*   **Lion**

required large amounts of food. They were swift runners and probably could catch almost anything that lived. They had enormous mouths filled with big, curved, daggerlike teeth, and their short, stout necks were extraordinarily strong. Their tails were long and powerful, like those of kangaroos, and when the carnosaurs ran, their tails extended straight out behind to balance the weight of their heavy bodies and huge heads. They walked on powerful, pillarlike hind legs that resembled those of a rhinoceros. Their feet looked somewhat like those of a chicken. Their arms were very short, and their fingers, as well as their toes, ended in great hooked claws.

Some scientists think carnosaurs must have been warm-blooded like modern birds and mammals because, they say, only warm-blooded animals could be such active hunters. Moreover, there seem to have been fewer of the big predators than of animals that were their prey. This is also true among birds and mammals living today. Among modern cold-blooded reptiles, however, there are equal numbers of predators and prey.

Scientists aren't sure what color the big meat-eaters were, but think they were probably dull greens, grays, or browns like large animals of today. Most predators succeed at stalking prey because their dull color camouflages them.

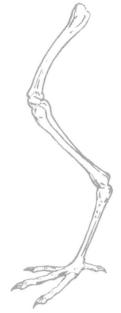

Chicken leg

Rhinoceros

Kangaroos

The largest and most powerful hunter among these Mesozoic monsters was *Tyrannosaurus rex* ("king of the tyrant lizards"). This was truly a fearsome creature. Its jaws were three feet long (longer than those of a hippopotamus) and filled with sixty gigantic curved teeth, some of which were six inches long. Both sides of every tooth were finely notched, like the serrated blade of a steak knife. Each tooth was very thick, and sharp as a dagger.

Tyrannosaurus's jaws were more powerful than those of any land predator that has ever lived. *Tyrannosaurus* could tear huge chunks from its prey—chunks as big as a full-grown goat—and easily swallow them whole.

This gigantic dinosaur was eighteen and a half feet tall, taller than most giraffes of today. It was as long as a big moving van. It could have looked over a one-story building without stretching. It was forty-five feet long from the tip of its snout to the end of its tail, and it weighed about five tons—more than two hippopotamuses.

Tyrannosaurus rex

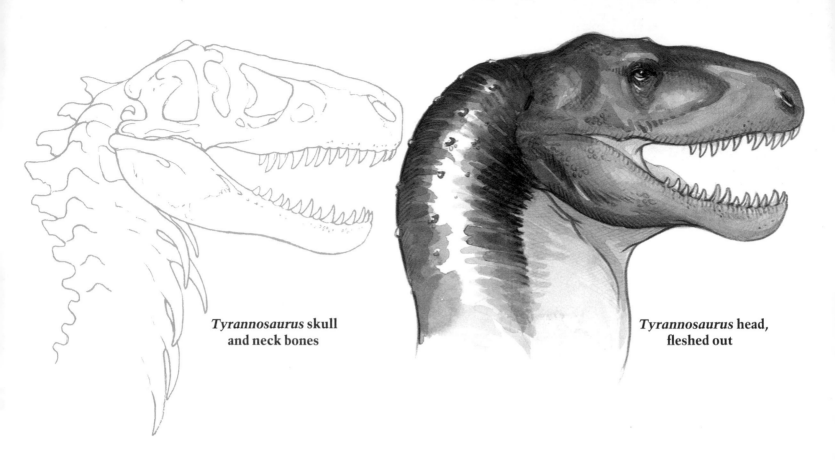

Tyrannosaurus skull and neck bones

Tyrannosaurus head, fleshed out

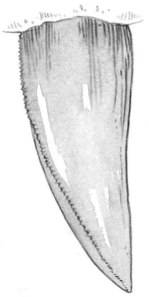

Tyrannosaurus tooth (actual length: 6 inches)

The "tyrant lizard" could catch and eat almost anything it wanted. It had no trouble sighting prey because its powerful neck carried its four-foot-long head well above its shoulders, giving it a good view of its surroundings. _Tyrannosaurus_ could judge space and distance well, too, because its eyes were in the front of its head. _Tyrannosaurus_ probably made lunging attacks with its jaws as it danced around its prey. Its foot and leg bones show that it could dodge well and, during counterattacks, could have avoided injury from the spikes and tail club of _Ankylosaurus_ and the horns of ceratopsians like _Triceratops_ or _Chasmosaurus_. Its three forward-pointing toes had sickle-shaped talons that were eight inches long—perfect for slicing meat.

Tyrannosaurus's hands had only two fingers, and its arms were so ridiculously short they couldn't reach its mouth (they were only thirty inches long). Its short arms must have been useful for something, though, because each finger had a long, strong claw. One theory suggests that the arms were used to help the creature stand up from a lying position. A low, thick ridge ran along the snout of male *Tyrannosaurus*. Scientists think this may mean that the males butted heads when fighting for mates.

Tyrannosaurus's hand

Tyrannosaurus getting up from lying position

These awesome creatures lived in western North America from about 70 to 65 million years ago. We know what they looked like because scientists have found five nearly complete *Tyrannosaurus rex* skeletons in Montana, Wyoming, New Mexico, and South Dakota.

Almost everyone has heard of *Tyrannosaurus*. It was one of the very last of the dinosaurs, but it was not the only monster of the Mesozoic. Scientists have found complete or nearly complete skeletons of fourteen

Two *Tyrannosaurus* and an ankylosaur

other carnosaurs and parts of at least twenty-five more. Ten of these looked a lot like *Tyrannosaurus rex* and, because they are apparently very close relatives, scientists place them all in the same family—the tyrannosaurid family. All of these dinosaurs had huge heads, pillarlike legs, very short arms, and two-fingered hands. They lived from 100 to 65 million years ago.

One of the tyrannosaurids, *Tarbosaurus bataar* ("alarming lizard from Bataar"), was a very close relative of *Tyrannosaurus*. It lived about the same time but in another part of the world. Thirteen *Tarbosaurus* skeletons were found in Mongolia (a part of Asia). This monster closely resembled "the tyrant lizard," except it was a little smaller and had a slightly longer skull. *Tarbosaurus* was forty-six feet long.

Like modern predators, *Tarbosaurus* probably ate whatever it could catch. It may have eaten dead animals it came across, too. Fossils of both *Tarbosaurus* and *Tyrannosaurus* were found near duckbill remains. They probably dined on duckbills often, even though these plant-eaters were not easy to catch. Although the carnosaurs were bigger and could run fast, the duckbills probably ran faster. The carnosaurs also preyed on the horned and armored dinosaurs, which were slow but well armed. If the big predators worked in teams, however, they most likely could have caught almost anything.

Tarbosaurus bataar chasing duckbills in a swamp

Albertosaurus libratus ("free lizard from Alberta") was king of the jungle in western Canada millions of years before *Tyrannosaurus*. This monster lived from 80 to 65 million years ago. It was not as large as *Tyrannosaurus* but was just as ugly and fearsome. *Albertosaurus* was thirty-three feet long and weighed about three tons. It was even more capable of slashing its victims than was *Tyrannosaurus*. Although its head was smaller than that of *Tyrannosaurus*, its arms and legs were longer. *Albertosaurus* probably could run faster and so may have been able to catch faster prey. A nearly complete adult and the remains of many juvenile *Albertosaurus* were found in Alberta, Canada.

Albertosaurus libratus running

Albertosaurus shared the jungle with another giant meat-eater, *Daspletosaurus torosus.* Its name means "frightful flesh-eating lizard," which is a good name for this creature. *Daspletosaurus* looked a lot like *Albertosaurus* but was a little shorter and stouter. It was only thirty feet long and weighed three and a half tons. *Daspletosaurus's* arms were longer than those of other members of the tyrannosaurid family. Its teeth were even larger than those of *Tyrannosaurus*, but there were fewer of them.

Daspletosaurus lived in marshy areas near streams and may have attacked the largest horned dinosaurs (ceratopsians) when they came to drink. This monster would have been difficult for a *Monoclonius* to shake loose once it had locked its jaws onto a shoulder or flank. Many kinds of horned dinosaurs were found near five *Daspletosaurus* skeletons discovered in Alberta, Canada.

Other members of the tyrannosaurid family, which are known only from small parts of the skull or skeleton, include *Alectrosaurus*, *Alioramus*, *Genyodectes*, *Indosuchus*, *Itemirus*, *Labocania*, and *Unquillosaurus*.

Daspletosaurus torosus attacking three **Monoclonius**

Other monsters lived even earlier than the earliest tyrannosaurids. Some of these were only distantly related to *Tyrannosaurus*, perhaps sharing a common ancestor. They are placed in different families. A nearly complete skeleton of one of these was found recently in England. It is called *Baryonyx walkeri* ("Walker's heavy strong claw"). It probably roamed all of northern Europe between 135 and 100 million years ago. This monster had a longer neck and arms than the tyrannosaurids but otherwise had a typical carnosaur body. It was thirty feet long, stood fourteen feet tall, and weighed about two tons. Its head, however, was quite different from those of all other carnosaurs. The snout of *Baryonyx* resembled that of a crocodile. It was long, narrow, and downturned, and was adorned with a triangular crest. *Baryonyx* had twice as many teeth as any other carnosaur; its jaws were lined with 128 finely serrated teeth.

Fish scales were found with *Baryonyx*'s remains. This suggests that *Baryonyx* may have been a fish-eater. It had at least one huge, twelve-inch claw that may have been used to snatch fish from the water.

Baronyx walkeri fishing

Spinosaurus aegypticus ("spiny lizard from Egypt") lived in northern Africa from 112 to 100 million years ago. This strange monster was nearly as large as *Tyrannosaurus*, but it was very different. It had extremely long spines—some up to six feet tall—on the vertebrae of its backbone. Scientists assume that the spines supported a sail of skin. The sail may have helped *Spinosaurus* keep cool, or it may have been used to attract mates.

This forty-foot-long carnosaur had serrated teeth, but they were straight rather than curved like those of most carnosaurs.

Similar spined dinosaurs include *Altispinax* and *Acrocanthosaurus*. *Altispinax* is known from only a few tall-spined vertebrae that were found in England.

Two *Spinosaurus aegypticus*

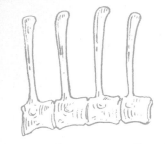

**Acrocanthosaurus atokensis's
high vertebral spines**

Acrocanthosaurus atokensis ("high-spined lizard from Atoka County, Oklahoma") is known from a large portion of the skeleton. It gets its name from the high vertebral spines—some up to seventeen inches long. Scientists think Acrocanthosaurus's spines supported extremely heavy muscles that were needed to carry the dinosaur's immense, thirty-five-inch head. They believe that Acrocanthosaurus carried its neck stretched out in front, unlike the tyrannosaurids, which walked with their necks curved back over their shoulders. The muscles probably formed a high ridge down the dinosaur's back. This monster was twelve feet tall and forty feet long. Its arms were longer than those of the tyrannosaurids. Scientists have not found evidence of its hands, but its

skull resembled those of earlier carnosaurs that had three-fingered hands.

Acrocanthosaurus may have hunted the Mesozoic forests in packs. Scientists discovered some eighteen-inch-long footprints in Texas, which they believe were made by fifteen different *Acrocanthosaurus*. Measurements of the strides indicate that these dinosaurs were running at twenty-five miles per hour. If they were chasing something, they very likely caught it. *Acrocanthosaurus* was probably one of the swiftest runners of all the carnosaurs. It lived in Texas and Oklahoma several million years before its cousin, *Tyrannosaurus*. Its closest ancestor may have been *Allosaurus*.

A herd of *Acrocanthosaurus* running

Allosaurus fragilis ("the brittle different lizard") is probably the second most familiar carnosaur. Scientists have discovered more skeletons of this carnosaur than any other. At least forty-four were found in one spot in Utah. These ranged in size from ten-foot-long juveniles to forty-five-foot-long adults, suggesting that *Allosaurus* may have lived in family groups. This fierce hunter lived in western North America from about 150 to 135 million years ago. It was about the same size as *Tyrannosaurus* and looked a lot like that dinosaur, but was more slender and had a smaller head, longer arms, and smaller teeth. Its head was three feet long, its arms were half as long as its hind legs, and its teeth were from two to four inches long.

An adult *Allosaurus* was forty-five feet long and up to sixteen and a half feet tall when standing erect. When it was running, its back was as high as an elephant's back. *Allosaurus*, like *Tyrannosaurus*, carried its huge head above its shoulders. Large windowlike openings in the skull reduced the head's weight.

This monster had good eyesight and may have been able to hunt in both dim light and bright sunshine. Its eyes were twice as large as those of any other carnosaur and they were shaded by low, bony crests along the brow. *Allosaurus* probably hunted many kinds of animals. Lots of *Camptosaurus*, *Stegosaurus*, and gigantic sauropods such as *Diplodocus*, *Apatosaurus*, and *Camarasaurus* lived nearby. Its teeth have been found with the remains of *Camarasaurus*, and tooth marks that exactly match its teeth were found on *Apatosaurus* tailbones. This is pretty good evidence that *Allosaurus* fed on these dinosaurs.

Scientists do not know whether *Allosaurus* actually killed these animals. A single *Allosaurus* probably could not have killed a healthy adult *Camarasaurus*. It may have eaten an already dead animal, or it may have been able to kill individuals that were sick or weakened by old age. We know from fossilized tracks that at least one *Allosaurus* stalked a large sauropod one day millions of years ago in Texas, but we don't know if *Allosaurus* caught the sauropod. These carnosaurs may have sometimes hunted in pairs or groups. Working together they would have been fearsome predators.

Allosaurus skull

Allosaurus fragilis and young

Other fossilized footprints tell us that this long-legged, nimble-footed dinosaur had a six-foot stride, which means it could have covered a lot of ground in a short time. It probably pranced around its prey and lunged in for bites at the neck or shoulder, or slashed at the belly with its talons. Its talons were even longer than those of *Tyrannosaurus*.

Allosaurus roamed the forests of a wide area that is now the Rocky Mountains.

Allosaurus stalking a sauropod

Although *Allosaurus* was probably a distant ancestor of *Tyrannosaurus*, it is placed in a different family, the allosaurid family. Allosaurids lived from 175 to 100 million years ago. All of them had longer arms than the tyrannosaurids, three-fingered hands, and large, narrow heads with windowlike openings in the skull. Two other allosaurids are known from nearly complete skeletons.

Yangchuanosaurus shangyouensis

Only the hands and feet are missing from two skeletons of *Yangchuanosaurus shangyouensis* ("lizard from Yang Ch'uan, China"). This monster lived in China from 150 to 140 million years ago. It closely resembled *Allosaurus*, but it was much smaller and its teeth were arranged differently. This allosaurid was twenty-six feet long. Its skull was thirty-two inches long. It probably ate just about anything it could catch.

The skeleton of a *Piatnitzkysaurus floresi* ("Piatnitzky's lizard") was found in Patagonia, Argentina. It lived from 175 to 165 million years ago, about 15 million years before *Allosaurus* roamed the earth. It may have been an ancestor of *Allosaurus*. It closely resembled *Allosaurus* but was smaller and had longer arms. *Piatnitzkysaurus* was between twenty and twenty-five feet long.

Fragmentary fossil evidence shows that other allosaurids lived in other parts of the world.

Piatnitzkysaurus *floresi* and young

Ceratosaurus nasicornis ("nose-horn horned lizard") lived at the same time as *Allosaurus* and in the same area, as well as in Africa. It resembled that dinosaur in many ways, and the two may have been closely related. *Ceratosaurus,* however, had four fingers on its hands and a horn on its nose. The horn was shaped somewhat like a rhinoceros's horn. No one knows what the horn was for. Perhaps it was used by males when fighting for mates. Some scientists think that *Ceratosaurus* may have had a thick ridge of muscles or a row of low, bony plates down its back.

Although *Ceratosaurus*'s skull was light, like that of *Allosaurus*, its head was smaller and shaped differently. This monster had heavy bony ridges above its eyes. Its teeth were delicate and thin, not at all like those of *Tyrannosaurus*. *Ceratosaurus*'s teeth more closely resembled those of *Allosaurus*, but there were fewer of them.

Two *Ceratosaurus nasicornis* feeding on a *Stegosaurus*

Ceratosaurus

Ceratosaurus was also smaller and perhaps weaker than *Allosaurus*. It was only twenty feet long (about as long as the pumper truck at the fire station) and six and a half feet tall at the hips. Nevertheless, this long-legged, nimble-footed monster was undoubtedly a powerful, savage hunter. Fossilized footprints show that it prowled the forests and marshes in packs. Its teeth, like those of *Allosaurus*, have been found with remains of *Camarasaurus*. Like most predators, it probably killed weak or young animals. It may also have eaten animals that died of other causes. As is true of all dinosaurs, it had an endless supply of teeth. When one fell out, another took its place.

Scientists found a nearly complete *Ceratosaurus* skeleton in Colorado and a partial skeleton in Tanzania, Africa.

The skull of a closely related monster called *Proceratosaurus* was found in Gloucestershire, England. This dinosaur also had a horn on its nose. It lived about the same time as *Piatnitzkysaurus* and was probably a forerunner of *Ceratosaurus*.

Proceratosaurus

Carnotaurus

Carnotaurus ("meat-eating bull") had two horns on its head. It was a strange-looking carnosaur. Although its forty-foot-long body was typical of all carnosaurs, its snout was short, and its two large horns resembled those of a bull. A nearly complete skeleton and some excellent skin impressions were found in Patagonia, Argentina, where it lived from about 75 to 65 million years ago. These impressions are the first skin impressions of a carnosaur ever found. They show that this dinosaur had rough, pebbly skin. *Abelisaurus*, a similar horned carnosaur, lived in the same area during the same period.

Eustreptospondylus oxoniensis ("Oxford's well-curved backbone") may have had a small horn on its nose, but this is not certain because part of the top of its skull is missing. The rest of the skeleton is complete

Eustreptospondylus oxoniensis

except for the hands. *Eustreptospondylus* was only twenty feet long and had smaller bones than most of the Mesozoic monsters. This carnosaur hunted in the forests of England and Madagascar from 146 to 135 million years ago. Scientists once thought it was a species of *Megalosaurus.* It is now known that, although *Eustreptospondylus* was a member of the same family (the megalosaurid family), it was a different dinosaur from *Megalosaurus. Eustreptospondylus* is the only megalosaurid known from a nearly complete skeleton.

Although a complete skeleton of *Megalosaurus bucklandi* ("Buckland's big lizard") has not yet been found, this animal is still important. Its fossils were among the first dinosaur fossils discovered, and it was the first dinosaur named. *Megalosaurus* was shorter than many carnosaurs, but it had bigger bones than most. Scientists believe this aggressive predator was twenty-five to thirty feet long and ten feet tall. It may have weighed two tons. It had a short, thick neck, massive hind legs, and very large eyes. Scientists think *Megalosaurus* and all members of its family carried their necks straight out rather than curved back over their shoulders.

Rows of tracks show that *Megalosaurus* ran in packs. It must have been the menace of the jungles of England and France, where from 180 to 135 million years ago it hunted large plant-eaters. *Megalosaurus* was a fast runner and probably attacked its prey with powerful jaws and daggerlike teeth.

Footprints found in Connecticut in 180-million-year-old rock may have been made by *Megalosaurus.* These footprints show that big carnosaurs could swim. These dinosaurs apparently floated on the surface of the water and kicked along the muddy bottom with the tips of their toes the way ostriches do today. This carnosaur may have been chasing prey or just cooling off.

Megalosaurus bucklandi swimming

Other members of the megalosaurid family are known only from fragmentary material. One of these, *Torvosaurus*, lived in western North America at the same time as *Allosaurus* and *Ceratosaurus*. *Torvosaurus* was more massive and had shorter arms than *Allosaurus* or *Ceratosaurus*, and may have been more closely related to *Tyrannosaurus*. *Torvosaurus*

Torvosaurus

Two *Camptosaurus*

Dryptosaurus

Chilantaisaurus

was about thirty-five feet long and may have weighed six tons. Each hand had three short fingers equipped with vicious-looking twelve-inch claws.

Other known megalosaurids lived between 180 and 90 million years ago. They roamed every continent except Antarctica. They include *Bahariasaurus*, *Carcharodontosaurus*, *Chilantaisaurus* (which had enormous hands with great hooked claws and a very thick skull), *Chingkankousaurus*, *Dryptosaurus*, *Erectopus*, *Gasosaurus*, *Indosaurus*, *Majungasaurus*, *Marshosaurus*, *Metriacanthosaurus*, *Piveteausaurus*, and *Sarcosaurus*.

The earliest known Mesozoic monster, *Dilophosaurus wetherilli* ("Wetherill's two-crested lizard"), hunted throughout southwestern North America around 200 million years ago. *Dilophosaurus* had a typical carnosaur body with a long tail, stout hind legs, and short, strong arms. Its hands had four fingers, but only three on each hand had long, sharp claws.

Dilophosaurus's neck, however, was longer and more flexible than the necks of other monsters. Its head, though large, was not as large as those of later carnosaurs. Two tall, thin crests, resembling halves of a dinner plate set on edge side by side, adorned its snout. The purpose of these crests is a mystery. They may have been used (like roosters' combs) to attract mates, or they may have served as temperature regulators. It is possible they served both purposes. They were too thin to be battering rams.

Dilophosaurus may have eaten animals it found already dead, but it was probably strong enough to kill *Anchisaurus*, a four-legged plant-eater that lived in its hunting range. It may have attacked victims with its long, curved talons. Although *Dilophosaurus* had long, sharp fangs, its jaws were too weak to allow it to kill prey with its teeth. Scientists think *Dilophosaurus* may have used its fangs to tear pieces of flesh from carcasses and then used its rear teeth to slice them up.

Several nearly complete skeletons of this great-granddaddy of *Tyrannosaurus rex* were found in northern Arizona. They were fifteen to twenty-five feet long.

Two *Dilophosaurus wetherilli*

Dilophosaurus attacking two *Anchisaurus*

44

Dilophosaurus was the first of the large group of dinosaurs that
dominated the earth for 135 million years. These monsters suddenly all died
out along with the other dinosaurs about 65 million years ago. No one
knows for sure why these magnificent creatures became extinct, but if they
hadn't, humans might never have become the dominant beings they are today.
Mammals did not become prominent until after the big meat-eaters were
no more.

WHEN THE CARNOSAURS LIVED

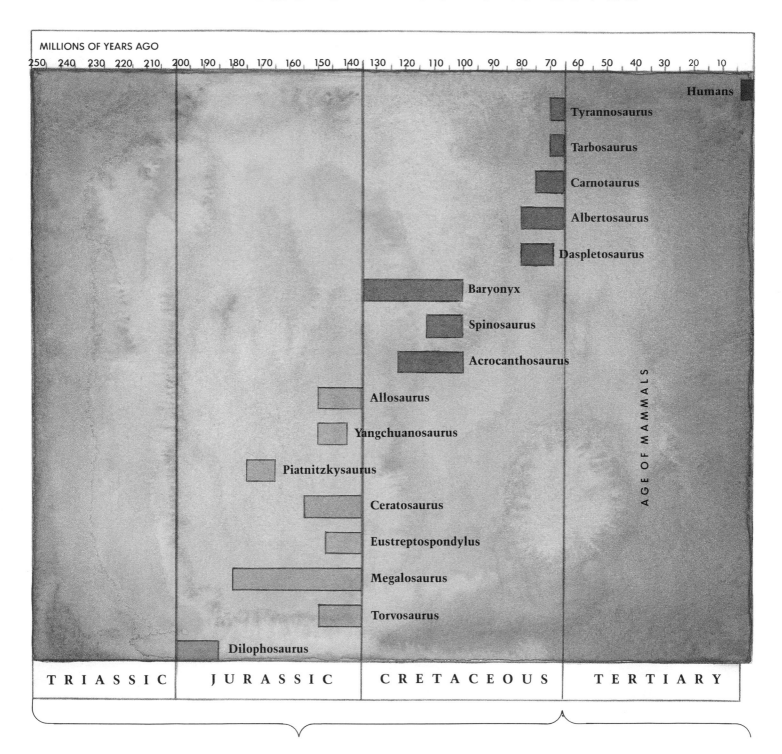

MILLIONS OF YEARS AGO
250 240 230 220 210 200 190 180 170 160 150 140 130 120 110 100 90 80 70 60 50 40 30 20 10

Humans

Tyrannosaurus

Tarbosaurus

Carnotaurus

Albertosaurus

Daspletosaurus

Baryonyx

Spinosaurus

Acrocanthosaurus

Allosaurus

Yangchuanosaurus

Piatnitzkysaurus

Ceratosaurus

Eustreptospondylus

Megalosaurus

Torvosaurus

Dilophosaurus

AGE OF MAMMALS

TRIASSIC   JURASSIC   CRETACEOUS   TERTIARY

MESOZOIC ERA   CENOZOIC ERA

PRONUNCIATION GUIDE AND INDEX
TO DINOSAURS IN THIS BOOK

FOR FURTHER READING

Bakker, Robert T. *The Dinosaur Heresies.* New York: William Morrow & Co., 1986.

Benton, Michael. *The Dinosaur Encyclopedia.* New York: Wanderer Books, 1984

Charig, Alan J. *A New Look at the Dinosaurs.* New York: Mayflower Books, 1979.

Colbert, Edwin H. *Dinosaurs an Illustrated History.* Maplewood, New Jersey: Hammond Incorporated, 1983.

Glut, Donald F. *The New Dinosaur Dictionary.* Secaucus, New Jersey: Citadel Press, 1982.

Norman, David. *The Illustrated Encyclopedia of Dinosaurs.* New York: Crescent Books, 1985.

Sattler, Helen Roney. *Dinosaurs of North America.* New York: Lothrop, Lee & Shepard Books, 1981.

Sattler, Helen Roney. *The Illustrated Dinosaur Dictionary.* New York: Lothrop, Lee & Shepard Books, 1983.